MW01093963

Sip-Deserving Boba Tea Recipes

Thirst-Quenching Boba Teas Better
Than Water

Table of Contents

Introduction

Boba or bubble tea isn't a façade of the millennium but one that existed from as far as the 1980s in Taiwan. At the time, elementary school children went by teashops after school to buy affordable and refreshing cups of tea after a hard day's work. As this became a regular practice, shop owners caught onto the trend and began opening cold teashops at various school locations to sell to kids.

Later on, one seller began improving her teas with different flavors and tea types, which would have other sellers catch onto the practice to compete against each other. The business was booming!

In 1983, Liu Han-Chieh, owner of Chin Shui Tang Teahouse, introduced the Japanese style of drinking cold coffee and used it to the preparation of tea-making in Taiwan. However, five years later, his staff Lin Hsiu Hui added her tapioca pudding into iced tea at a meeting, and there, a new idea was birth for the company. The result of the tea creating a bubble-like effect at the bottom and top of the tea fascinated the owner, staff, and customers, which made it a top purchase for the company.

On and on, many recipe developers like me have caught on to this amazing invention and have sort varying ways to flavor up boba teas. There has been a focus to integrate boba tea into many cultures while using local ingredients specific to different regions to reach this goal.

This cookbook is an assemblage of some of my best results yet as I crack further into the codes of boba teas for more reveals. I share thirty recipes that are natural to make and use easily accessible ingredients. They are nourishing enough to make you create more and more cups.

I know you are ready to start making your favorite cups, so that I wouldn't hold you any further.

Disclaimer: However, most importantly, make sure to use straws when sipping the teas as tapioca pearls tend to be swallowed. This can become a throat hazard.

Now, let's jump in!

1. Classic Boba Tea

A basic that has originated from time immemorial and is enjoyed to this date.

Serving: 2

Prep Time: 5 mins

Cooking Time: 7 mins + 2 hours chilling

Ingredients:

- 1 cup black jumbo tapioca pearls
- 2 cups freshly brewed strong black tea
- 2 tbsp brown sugar
- Ice cubes
- 1 cup whole milk

Instructions:

1. Bring 4 cups of water to a boil in a large pot over medium heat. Add the tapioca pearls, quickly stir to prevent sticking, and allow them cook for 5 to 7 minutes or until floated to the top. Drain through a colander and run cold water over the pearls immediately. Set aside.

2. In a pitcher, mix the tea and brown sugar until the sugar dissolves. Place the jar in the refrigerator and chill for 2 hours.

3. To serve, divide the tapioca pearls into 2 large drinking glasses. Top with the ice cubes, then the tea and milk.

4. Stir, insert boba straws, and serve.

2. Strawberry Vanilla Boba Tea

Two power flavors combined in one creamy cup of tea.

Serving: 2

Prep Time: 5 mins

Cooking Time: 7 minutes

Ingredients:

- 1 cup black jumbo tapioca pearls
- 1 cup frozen vanilla yogurt
- 1 cup fresh strawberries, chopped

- 1 cup ice cubes
- 1 cup whole milk

Instructions:

1. Cook the tapioca pearls in 3 cups of boiling water until floated to the top, 5 to 7 minutes. Drain through a colander and run cold water on top. Set aside to keep draining.

2. In a blender, add the vanilla yogurt, strawberries, ice cubes, and milk. Process until smooth.

3. To serve, divide the tapioca pearls between 2 drinking glasses and pour the drink on top.

4. Insert boba straws and serve immediately.

3. Mango Boba Tea

A sunshine color that is right for summer.

Serving: 2

Prep Time: 5 mins

Cooking Time: 7 minutes

Ingredients:

- 1 cup black jumbo tapioca pearls
- 1 cup ice cubes
- 1 cup mango juice

- 1 cup fresh mango, chopped
- 1 cup whole milk

Instructions:

1. Cook the tapioca pearls in 3 cups of boiling water until floated to the top, 5 to 7 minutes. Drain through a colander, run cold water on top and set aside to keep draining.

2. Meanwhile, in a blender, add the ice cubes, mango juice, mango, and milk. Process until smooth.

3. To serve, divide the tapioca pearls into 2 drinking glasses and top with the drink.

4. Insert boba straws and serve immediately.

4. Peanut Boba Tea

I love the nuttiness that goes on here, which makes it perfect for a breakfast drink.

Serving: 2

Prep Time: 5 mins

Cooking Time: 7 minutes

Ingredients:

- 1 cup black jumbo tapioca pearls
- ¼ cup peanut butter
- 1 cup unsweetened soymilk

- 3 tbsp honey
- 1 cup freshly brewed black tea, room temperature
- 1 cup ice cubes

Instructions:

1. Add the tapioca pearls to 3 cups of boiling water, stir and cook until floated to the top of the water, 5 to 7 minutes. Drain through a colander, run cold water on top and set aside to keep draining.

2. In a blender, add the peanut butter, ice cubes, soymilk, honey, and black tea. Process until smooth.

3. To serve, divide the tapioca pearls between 2 drinking glasses and top with the tea mixture.

4. Insert boba straws and serve immediately.

5. Avocado Boba Tea

It is thick and nice on the tongue.

Serving: 2

Prep Time: 7 mins

Cooking Time: 7 mins + 2-hour chilling time

Ingredients:

- ¼ cup tapioca pearl
- 2 cups prepared green tea, room temperature

- 2 medium soft avocados, pitted and peeled
- 2 tbsp maple syrup
- 2 tbsp white sugar

Instructions:

1. Cook the tapioca pearls in 3 cups of boiling water for 5 to 7 minutes or until floated to the top of the water. Drain through a colander and run cold water over. Set aside to drain.

2. Meanwhile, in a blender, add the green tea, avocados, maple syrup, and sugar. Blend until smooth. Pour the mixture into a jar and chill for at least 2 hours.

3. To serve, divide the tapioca pearls between 2 drinking glasses and pour the tea on top.

4. Insert boba straws and serve immediately.

6. Thai Boba Tea

Something from the camp of Thailand.

Serving: 2

Prep Time: 5 mins

Cooking Time: 7 mins + 2 hours chilling

Ingredients:

- 1 cup black jumbo tapioca pearls
- 2 cups Thai tea mix
- ½ cup granulated sugar
- 1/2 cup coconut milk

Instructions:

1. Cook the tapioca pearls in 3 cups of boiling water over medium heat until floated to the top of the water, 5 to 7 minutes. Drain through a colander, run cold water on top and set aside to keep draining.

2. In a large jug, mix the Thai tea, sugar, and coconut milk until the sugar dissolves. Place the drink in the refrigerator and chill for at least 2 hours.

3. To serve, divide the tapioca pearls between 2 drinking glasses, remove and stir the drink, and pour over the tapioca pearls.

4. Insert boba straws and serve immediately.

7. Jasmine Boba Tea

With jasmine tea bags, you can create a whole new vibe to your tea glasses!

Serving: 2

Prep Time: 5 mins

Cooking Time: 17 minutes + 2 hours chilling

Ingredients:

- 6 to 8 jasmine tea bags
- 1 cup clear jumbo tapioca pearls
- 4 tbsp granulated sugar
- 1 cup unsweetened almond milk

Instructions:

1. Cook the tapioca pearls in 3 cups of boiling water over medium heat until floated to the top of the water, 5 to 7 minutes. Drain through a colander, run cold water all over the pearls and set aside to keep draining.

2. Steep the tea bags in 2 cups of boiling water for 10 minutes and remove the bags afterward. Allow complete cooling and mix in the sugar and almond milk until dissolves. Transfer the drink into a large jug and chill in the refrigerator for 2 hours.

3. To serve, divide the tapioca pearls between 2 drinking glasses and pour the drink on top.

4. Insert boba straws and serve immediately.

8. Matcha Boba Tea

Matcha and tea are an item and must be fully embraced. That's what happens here!

Serving: 2

Prep Time: 5 mins

Cooking Time: 7 minutes + 1-hour chilling

Ingredients:

- 1 cup black jumbo tapioca pearls
- 2 tbsp matcha powder
- 1 ½ cups whole milk
- 2 tbsp granulated sugar

Instructions:

1. Cook the tapioca pearls in 3 cups of boiling water over medium heat until floated to the top of the water, 5 to 7 minutes. Drain through a colander, run cold water all over the pearls and set aside to keep draining.

2. Combine the matcha powder, milk, and sugar in a jug and chill in the refrigerator for 1 hour.

3. To serve, divide the tapioca pearls between 2 drinking glasses and top with the chilled tea.

4. Insert boba straws and serve immediately.

9. English Breakfast Boba Tea

Don't have your morning English tea as it is any longer. Transform it into this boba tea and enjoy it better.

Serving: 2

Prep Time: 5 mins

Cooking Time: 10 mins + 1-hour chilling

Ingredients:

- 1 cup black jumbo tapioca pearls
- 4 English breakfast tea bags
- 2 tbsp granulated sugar
- 1 cup whole milk

Instructions:

1. Cook the tapioca pearls in 3 cups of boiling water over medium heat until floated to the top of the water, 5 to 7 minutes. Drain through a colander, run cold water all over the pearls and set aside to keep draining.

2. Meanwhile, steep the tea bags in 3 cups of hot water for 10 minutes. Remove the bags and allow complete cooling. After, mix in the sugar until dissolved and then, the milk. Chill the tea in the refrigerator for 1 hour.

3. To serve, divide the tapioca pearls between 2 drinking glasses and top with the tea.

4. Insert boba straws and serve immediately.

10. Kiwi Citrus Boba Tea

What an aromatic, tropical blend perfect for the summer too!

Serving: 2

Prep Time: 5 mins

Cooking Time: 7 mins

Ingredients:

- 1 cup black jumbo tapioca pearls
- 1 cup steeped plain tea, cooled
- 1 cup orange juice
- 3 medium kiwifruits, peeled
- 2 tbsp granulated sugar
- Ice cubes for serving

Instructions:

1. Cook the tapioca pearls in 3 cups of boiling water over medium heat until floated to the top of the water, 5 to 7 minutes. Drain through a colander, run cold water all over the pearls and set aside to keep draining.

2. In a blender, combine the tea, orange juice, kiwis, and sugar. Process until smooth.

3. To serve, divide the tapioca pearls into 2 glasses, top with the ice cubes, and then the drink.

4. Insert boba straws and serve immediately.

11. Blueberry Boba Tea

Right for the early afternoon when in search of a chilled drink to calm your busy body.

Serving: 2

Prep Time: 5 mins

Cooking Time: 7 mins

Ingredients:

- 1 cup black jumbo tapioca pearls
- 1 cup steep green tea, cooled
- ½ cup frozen blueberries
- 3 tbsp granulated sugar
- ½ cup whole milk
- Ice cubes for serving

Instructions:

1. Cook the tapioca pearls in 3 cups of boiling water over medium heat until floated to the top of the water, 5 to 7 minutes. Drain through a colander, run cold water all over the pearls and set aside to keep draining.

2. In a blender, add the tea, blueberries, sugar, and milk. Process until smoothly combined.

3. To serve, divide the tapioca pearls, ice cubes, and drink into 2 drinking glasses.

4. Insert boba straws and serve immediately.

12. Watermelon Strawberry Boba Tea

A flavor and color that reminds us of the early days of summer.

Serving: 2

Prep Time: 5 mins

Cooking Time: 7 mins

Ingredients:

- 1 cup black jumbo tapioca pearls
- 2 cups steeped English tea bags, cooled
- 1 cup frozen strawberries
- ½ cup chopped frozen watermelon
- Ice cubes for serving

Instructions:

1. Cook the tapioca pearls in 3 cups of boiling water over medium heat until floated to the top of the water, 5 to 7 minutes. Drain through a colander, run cold water all over the pearls and set aside to keep draining.

2. Combine the tea, strawberries, and watermelon in blender and process until smooth.

3. To serve, divide the tapioca pearls and ice cubes into 2 drinking glasses and top with the drink.

4. Insert boba straws and serve immediately.

13. Grape Boba Tea

When not up of white wine, I substitute with this grape drink. It is always satisfying.

Serving: 2

Prep Time: 5 mins

Cooking Time: 7 mins

Ingredients:

- 1 cup jumbo black tapioca pearls
- 1 cup steeped plain tea
- 1 cup red grape juice

- 2 tbsp granulated sugar
- Ice cubes for serving

Instructions:

1. Cook the tapioca pearls in 3 cups of boiling water over medium heat until floated to the top of the water, 5 to 7 minutes. Drain through a colander, run cold water all over the pearls and set aside to keep draining.

2. In a jar, mix the tea, grape juice, and sugar until the sugar dissolves.

3. Divide the tapioca into 2 drinking glasses, top with the ice cubes and pour the drink on top.

4. Insert boba straws and serve immediately.

14. Spiced Orange Boba Tea

How cool a combination –orange with ginger? You will love the blend.

Serving: 2

Prep Time: 5 mins

Cooking Time: 7 mins

Ingredients:

- 1 cup black jumbo tapioca pearls
- 1 cup steeped plain white tea, cooled

- 1 cup orange juice
- ¼ tsp ginger powder
- 3 tbsp maple syrup
- ½ tsp vanilla extract
- 5 tbsp unsweetened coconut milk
- Ice cubes for serving

Instructions:

1. Cook the tapioca pearls in 3 cups of boiling water over medium heat until floated to the top of the water, 5 to 7 minutes. Drain through a colander, run cold water all over the pearls and set aside to keep draining.

2. In a large jug, mix the tea, orange juice, maple syrup, vanilla, and coconut milk.

3. To serve, divide the tapioca pearls between 2 drinking glasses. Top with the ice cubes and pour the drink on top.

4. Insert boba straws and serve immediately.

15. Ginger-Cardamom Boba Tea

We appreciate the Indian cuisine for this addition. Ginger and cardamom are typical Indian spices used for many foods and drinks alike.

Serving: 2

Prep Time: 10 mins

Cooking Time: 19 minutes

Ingredients:

- 1 cup black jumbo tapioca pearls
- 1 small cinnamon stick

- 2 cardamom pods, split open
- ½-inch ginger root, peeled and thinly sliced
- 4 black teabags
- 4 tbsp honey
- 1 cup coconut milk
- Ice cubes for serving

Instructions:

1. Cook the tapioca pearls in 3 cups of boiling water over medium heat until floated to the top of the water, 5 to 7 minutes. Drain through a colander, run cold water all over the pearls and set aside to keep draining.

2. Meanwhile, pour 2 cups of water in a medium pot and add the cinnamon stick, cardamom pods, and ginger. Bring to a boil over medium heat and turn the heat off. Add the tea bags and allow steeping for 10 minutes. Strain the solids from the liquids, stir in the honey, coconut milk, and set aside to cool completely.

3. To serve, divide the tapioca pearls between 2 drinking glasses, top with the ice cubes and then, the drink.

4. Insert boba straws and serve immediately.

16. Melon Boba Tea

How often do we incorporate melon in foods? Rarely, however, here is an option to appreciate the beauty of melons better.

Serving: 2

Prep Time: 5 mins

Cooking Time: 7 mins

Ingredients:

- 1 cup black jumbo tapioca pearls
- 2 cups steeped green tea, cooled
- 3 tbsp granulated sugar
- 3 cups chopped melon
- Ice cubes for serving

Instructions:

1. Cook the tapioca pearls in 3 cups of boiling water over medium heat until floated to the top of the water, 5 to 7 minutes. Drain through a colander, run cold water all over the pearls and set aside to keep draining.

2. In a blender, combine the green tea, sugar, and melon. Process until smooth.

3. To serve, divide the tapioca pearls between 2 drinking glasses, add the ice cubes, and pour the drink on top.

4. Insert boba straws and serve immediately.

17. Chai Boba Tea

Chai tea originates from India too, and requires nothing more than chai tea bags and some milk to make this drink.

Serving: 2

Prep Time: 5 mins

Cooking Time: 7 mins

Ingredients:

- 1 cup black jumbo tapioca pearls
- 2 cups steeped chai tea
- 1 cup coconut milk
- 4 tbsp honey
- Ice cubes for serving

Instructions:

1. Cook the tapioca pearls in 3 cups of boiling water until floated to the top of the water, 5 to 7 minutes. Drain, run cold water on top and set aside.

2. In a jug, mix the chai tea, coconut milk, and honey.

3. To serve, divide the tapioca pearls between 2 glasses, add the ice cubes, and pour the tea on top.

4. Insert boba straws and serve immediately.

18. Coconut Vanilla Boba Tea

A shout-out to coconut milk and its excellent health benefits.
This mixture is a high recommendation for you.

Serving: 2

Prep Time: 5 mins

Cooking Time: 7 mins + 2 hours chilling

Ingredients:

- 1 cup black jumbo tapioca pearls
- 2 cups steeped black tea
- 1 tsp vanilla extract
- 1 cup coconut milk
- 3 tbsp honey

Instructions:

1. Cook the tapioca pearls in 3 cups of boiling water until floated to the top of the water, 5 to 7 minutes. Drain, run cold water on top and set aside.

2. In a jug, mix the tea, vanilla, coconut milk, and honey. Chill in the refrigerator for 2 hours.

3. To serve, divide the tapioca pearls between 2 glasses and pour the tea on top.

4. Insert boba straws and serve immediately.

19. Taro Boba Tea

Taro, also known as cocoyam is a classic ingredient for making boba tea in most parts of Asia. Make sure to use treated taro powder for this recipe to avoid food poisoning.

Serving: 2

Prep Time: 10 mins

Cooking Time: 7 mins

Ingredients:

- 1 cup black jumbo tapioca pearls
- 3 tbsp taro grade-A powder
- 3 tbsp granulated sugar
- 3 tbsp almond milk
- 1 ¾ cup water
- Ice cubes for serving

Instructions:

1. Cook the tapioca pearls in 3 cups of boiling water until floated to the top of the water, 5 to 7 minutes. Drain, run cold water on top and set aside.

2. In a blender, combine the taro powder, sugar, almond milk, and water. Process until smooth.

3. To serve, divide the tapioca pearls between 2 glasses, top with the ice and pour the drink on top.

4. Insert boba straws and serve immediately.

20. Raspberry Banana Boba Tea

A thick and nourishing drink to silence those hunger pangs in the early afternoon hours.

Serving: 2

Prep Time: 10 mins

Cooking Time: 7 mins

Ingredients:

- 1 cup black jumbo tapioca pearls
- 2 cups steeped plain tea, cooled
- 1 cup frozen raspberries
- ½ banana, peeled and chopped
- Sugar to taste
- Ice cubes for serving

Instructions:

1. Cook the tapioca pearls in 3 cups of boiling water over medium heat until floated to the top of the water, 5 to 7 minutes. Drain through a colander, run cold water all over the pearls and set aside to keep draining.

2. Combine the tea, raspberries, banana, and sugar in a blender, and process until smooth.

3. To serve, divide the tapioca pearls and ice cubes into 2 drinking glasses and top with the drink.

4. Insert boba straws and serve immediately.

21. Vietnamese Iced Coffee Boba Tea

The item of shine here is the condensed milk that offers the drink a peculiar aroma distinct to Vietnamese cuisine.

Serving: 2

Prep Time: 5 mins

Cooking Time: 7 mins

Ingredients:

- 1 cup black jumbo tapioca pearls
- 1 cup freshly made espresso, cooled
- ½ cup honey
- 2 tbsp condensed milk
- Ice cubes for serving

Instructions:

1. Cook the tapioca pearls in 3 cups of boiling water until floated to the top of the water, 5 to 7 minutes. Drain the tapioca pearls through a colander, run cold water over, and set aside to drain.

2. Meanwhile, in a large jug, mix the coffee, honey, and condensed milk.

3. To serve, divide the tapioca pearls between 2 drinking glasses, add the ice cubes and pour the drink on top.

4. Insert boba straws and serve immediately.

22. Red Bean Boba Tea

Grab some sweet red bean paste and make rich, satisfying drink out of it.

Serving: 2

Prep Time: 5 mins

Cooking Time: 7 mins + 1-hour chilling

Ingredients:

- 1 cup black jumbo tapioca pearls
- 2/3 cup sweet red bean paste
- 3 cups coconut milk
- 2 tbsp water
- 2 tbsp honey

Instructions:

1. Cook the tapioca pearls in 3 cups of boiling water over medium heat until floated to the top of the water, 5 to 7 minutes. Drain through a colander, run cold water all over the pearls and set aside to keep draining.

2. In a blender, add the red bean paste, coconut milk, water, and honey. Process until smooth. Pour the mixture into a jug and chill in the refrigerator for 45 minutes to 1 hour.

3. To serve, divide the tapioca pearls between 2 drinking glasses and pour the drink on top.

4. Insert boba straws and serve immediately.

23. Cream Cheese Boba Tea

A mouthful of creaminess is what your get from these cups.

Serving: 2

Prep Time: 10 mins

Cooking Time: 7 mins + 30 mins chilling

Ingredients:

- 1 cup black jumbo tapioca pearls
- 1 cup heavy cream
- ¼ cup condensed milk
- ¼ cup softened cream cheese
- 2 tbsp granulated sugar
- 2 cups steeped green tea, cooled
- Ice cubes for serving
- ½ tsp salt
- ¼ tsp cocoa powder

Instructions:

1. Cook the tapioca pearls in 3 cups of boiling water over medium heat until floated to the top of the water, 5 to 7 minutes. Drain through a colander, run cold water all over the pearls and set aside to keep draining.

2. In a medium bowl, using an electric hand mixer, whisk the heavy cream, condensed milk, cream cheese, and sugar until soft peaks form. Chill in the refrigerator for 30 minutes.

3. To serve, divide the tapioca between 2 drinking glasses, top with the ice cubes and pour in the drink, two-thirds way

up. Remove the cheese mixture from the fridge and spoon onto the tea to the brim. Sprinkle the top with salt and then the cocoa powder.

4. Carefully insert boba straws and serve immediately.

24. Lychee Yogurt Boba Tea

Lychee is one of my favorite fruits, which in combination with Greek yogurt offers a unique flavor.

Serving: 2

Prep Time: 5 mins

Cooking Time: 7 mins

Ingredients:

- 1 cup black jumbo tapioca pearls
- 3 cups steeped plain tea, cooled
- 6 pieces lychee, peeled, chopped and frozen

- ¼ cup lychee syrup
- ¼ cup Greek yogurt
- Ice cubes for serving

Instructions:

1. Cook the tapioca pearls in 3 cups of boiling water over medium heat until floated to the top of the water, 5 to 7 minutes. Drain through a colander, run cold water all over the pearls and set aside to keep draining.

2. In a blender, combine the tea, lychee, lychee syrup, and yogurt. Process until smooth.

3. To serve, divide the tapioca pearls between 2 drinking glasses, add the ice cubes, and pour the drink on top.

4. Insert boba straws and serve immediately.

25. Iced Fruit Boba Tea

Grab your favorite tropical fruits and combine them into this tea. It is a lovely taste to enjoy.

Serving: 2

Prep Time: 5 mins

Cooking Time: 7 mins

Ingredients:

- 1 cup black jumbo tapioca pearls
- 2 cups tropical fruit juice, cold
- 1 cup steeped plain tea, cooled
- ¼ cup frozen finely chopped peach

- ¼ cup frozen raspberries

Instructions:

1. Cook the tapioca pearls in 3 cups of boiling water over medium heat until floated to the top of the water, 5 to 7 minutes. Drain through a colander, run cold water all over the pearls and set aside to keep draining.

2. In a large jug, mix the fruit juice and tea.

3. To serve, divide the tapioca pearls between 2 drinking glasses, drop in the peaches, raspberries, and pour the drink on top.

4. Insert boba straws and serve immediately.

26. Passion Fruit Boba Tea

I love the subtle flavor of passion fruit a lot, which makes this tea one of my favorites.

Serving: 2

Prep Time: 5 mins

Cooking Time: 7 mins

Ingredients:

- 1 cup black jumbo tapioca pearls
- 2 cups steeped black tea, chilled
- 10 passion fruits, pulp extracted
- 1 cup passion fruit juice, chilled
- 3 tbsp maple syrup
- Ice cubes for serving

Instructions:

1. Cook the tapioca pearls in 3 cups of boiling water over medium heat until floated to the top of the water, 5 to 7 minutes. Drain through a colander, run cold water all over the pearls and set aside to keep draining.

2. In a blender, add the black tea and passion fruit extract. Blend until the passion fruits are well crushed. Strain the mixture through a fine-mesh into a jug. Stir in the passion fruit juice and maple syrup until well combined.

3. To serve, divide the tapioca pearls between 2 drinking glasses, top with the ice cube, and pour the drink on top.

4. Insert boba straws and serve immediately.

27. Just Vanilla Boba Tea

Do you like vanilla flavor a lot like me? Then, you will like this light tea loaded with vanilla.

Serving: 2

Prep Time: 5 mins

Cooking Time: 7 mins

Ingredients:

- 1 cup jumbo tapioca pearls
- 3 cups brewed vanilla tea, chilled

- 2 cups water
- 1/3 cup granulated sugar

Instructions:

1. Cook the tapioca pearls in 3 cups of boiling water over medium heat until floated to the top of the water, 5 to 7 minutes. Drain through a colander, run cold water all over the pearls and set aside to keep draining.

2. In a jug, mix the tea, water, and sugar.

3. To serve, divide the tapioca pearls into 2 drinking glasses, add the ice cubes, and top with the tea.

4. Insert boba straws and serve immediately.

28. Granny Smith Boba Tea

Grab as many Granny Smith apples as you like and blend them into tea for your loved ones and you.

Serving: 2

Prep Time: 5 mins

Cooking Time: 7 mins

Ingredients:

- 1 cup black jumbo tapioca pearls
- 8 Granny Smith apples, cored, chopped and frozen
- 3 cups steeped plain tea, chilled
- 3 tbsp granulated sugar
- Ice cubes for serving

Instructions:

1. Cook the tapioca pearls in 3 cups of boiling water over medium heat until floated to the top of the water, 5 to 7 minutes. Drain through a colander, run cold water all over the pearls and set aside to keep draining.

2. In a blender, add 1 cup of the tea and the apples. Process until smooth and thick. Pour in the remaining tea and sugar. Continue blending until well combined.

3. To serve, divide the tapioca pearls and ice cubes between 2 drinking glasses and pour the drink on top.

4. Insert boba straws and serve immediately.

29. Lavender Boba Tea

Who would have thought that lavender would work out well in a cup of tea? It is terrific how culinary lavender creates a beautiful aroma in this tea.

Serving: 2

Prep Time: 5 mins

Cooking Time: 17 mins + 1-hour chilling

Ingredients:

- 1 cup black jumbo tapioca pearls
- 3 lavender tea bags
- 1 cup whole milk
- 3 tbsp granulated sugar
- Ice cubes for serving

Instructions:

1. Cook the tapioca pearls in 3 cups of boiling water over medium heat until floated to the top of the water, 5 to 7 minutes. Drain through a colander, run cold water all over the pearls and set aside to keep draining.

2. Meanwhile, steep the lavender tea bags in 2 cups of freshly boiled water. Allow sitting for 7 to 10 minutes to steep. Remove the tea bags, allow complete cooling and mix in the milk, and sugar. Chill the tea for 1 hour.

3. To serve, divide the tapioca pearls and ice cubes between 2 drinking glasses and pour the tea on top.

4. Insert boba straws and serve immediately.

30. Chocolate Boba Tea

And the best had to be saved for the last. I know you would love this drink and everyone else.

Serving: 2

Prep Time: 5 mins

Cooking Time: 7 mins + 1 hour

Ingredients:

- 1 cup black jumbo tapioca pearls
- 2 tbsp sweetened cocoa powder
- 2 cups whole milk
- 1 cup hot water
- Ice cubes for serving
- Whipping cream for topping
- Chocolate chips to garnish

Instructions:

1. Cook the tapioca pearls in 3 cups of boiling water over medium heat until floated to the top of the water, 5 to 7 minutes. Drain through a colander, run cold water all over the pearls and set aside to keep draining.

2. In a jug, mix the milk, water and cocoa powder until smooth. Allow complete cooling and chill the tea for 1 hour.

3. To serve, divide the tapioca pearls between 2 drinking glasses, top with the ice and the drink two-thirds way up. Swirl some whipping cream on the drink and garnish with the chocolate chips.

4. Insert boba straws and serve immediately.

Conclusion

After all these beautiful recipes have been shared, do you know which are your favorites?

How do you plan to spread your new love for boba teas? Will you be making them and sharing them with the family? Or will you host frequent, mini boba tea parties to treat your friends to a good feeling?

I believe whatever your choice, you'll have a fun time at it.

I'm heading onto my next book, and until we meet soon, I wish you a fantastic time!

Cheers!

Made in the USA
Las Vegas, NV
02 January 2024

83827551R00039